Mary's

LUKE 1:5 – 2:18 FOR CHILDREN

Written by M. M. Brem
Illustrated by Sally Mathews

ARCH® Books

© 1967 CONCORDIA PUBLISHING HOUSE, ST. LOUIS, MISSOURI

MANUFACTURED IN THE UNITED STATES OF AMERICA
ISBN 0-570-06029-X

One day as Mary washed her clothes,
she had a sudden scare.
And how she jumped! She was surprised
to see an angel there.

Before she had a chance to speak,
the angel said, "Don't fear.
I have important news for you.
Our God has sent me here.

"For you will have a baby soon,
and He will be God's Son.
His name is Jesus. He will come
in love for everyone."

"But I'm not married yet," she said.
"So how can this be true?"
"That isn't hard for God," he said.
"There's nothing He can't do.

"He'll send the Holy Spirit down.
But that's not all God's done.
For though Elizabeth is old,
she, too, will have a son."

And Mary said, "It's wonderful
that I may serve the Lord.
Whatever God wants, I will do
according to His Word."

And when the angel disappeared
then Mary packed to go.
"The angel told me what to do.
I know where I will go.

"I'll go and see Elizabeth;
it's just the thing to do.
And I would like to know if she
has seen the angel too."

She said, "Good-by," and hurried off.
It was not long before
Elizabeth heard Mary knock.
She hurried to the door.

Elizabeth saw Mary there.
Her heart was filled with joy.
"Great wonders have been done," she said,
"I, too, will have a boy!

"Our God has blessed us both," she said,
"but you're the honored one.
You are the one God chose to be
the mother of His Son."

And Mary sang a song of praise.
"Lord, I believe that You
will send Your Son to save us as
You promised You would do."

That night they sat and talked
when there
was nothing else to do.
And Mary said, "I wondered if
you saw the angel too."

Elizabeth said, "No, not I!
He did not come to me!
But Zechariah was the one
the angel came to see.

"An angel suddenly appeared
quite close to where he stood,
and Zechariah shook with fear
as anybody would.

"The angel said, 'Don't be afraid.
I have good news for you.
You know that you are very old
and that your wife is too.

" 'But God has a surprise for you,
a very special one.
Our God decided it is time
to give you both a son.

" 'You'll call him John. He will prepare
the people for God's Son.
He'll baptize men and preach *good news*
and say, "God's Son is come!" ' "

"My husband said, 'How will I know
the things you say are true?'
The sign the angel gave is why
he cannot talk to you."

And Mary stayed with them three months.

But then she said one day,
    "It's time for me to go back home.

I should be on my way."

She said, "Good-by," and hurried home.
When Joseph married her,
he said, "Now we must make our home,
so where would you prefer?"

"Let's stay right here," she said. But God
had other plans for them,
and so He had them leave their home
and go to Bethlehem.

The town was crowded,
rooms were scarce
when they arrived that day.

A stable was the only place
where both of them could stay.

And late that night God's Son was born,
and Jesus was His name.
But everyone in town slept on
and didn't know He came.

Some shepherds were the first to know.
While tending sheep that night,
an angel suddenly they saw.
The hills were bright with light.

"Don't be afraid," the angel said.
"Just go to Bethlehem,
and you will find your Savior there.
Now go and worship Him."

"He's come!" one said. "The Savior whom
we've waited for is here!"
"Let's go and see!" another said.
"That town is very near."

More angels came to them before
they went to Bethlehem.
"Glory be to God on high!"
the angels sang to them.

"Peace on earth! Goodwill to men!
God's Son has come to earth!"
After that they went and found
the place of Jesus' birth.

They found the stable where He was
and quietly went in
to worship Jesus, who had come
to save us from our sin.

DEAR PARENTS:

The birth of Jesus is the central point of the familiar Christmas Gospel, but St. Luke tells us that some wonderful things happened before He was born in the stable in Bethlehem.

The angel messenger paid a surprise visit to the maiden Mary and announced that she would bear the promised Son. When she questioned how this could be, the angel gave the answer: The Holy Spirit would come and make it possible for her to conceive, for God can do anything. In childlike faith young Mary accepted the Word of the Lord and promised to be His servant.

Bursting to share the news, she hurried to visit her cousin Elizabeth. Can you imagine their excitement as they discussed the wonders of God? Elizabeth would become the mother of John the Baptist, and Mary would give birth to the promised Savior.

Will you help your child see the wonder of God's grace in choosing a humble maid to be the mother of Jesus? Will you lead him to see the joy of Mary in believing the Word of God and in doing what He asked? Above all, will you share the Good News that Jesus Christ is born to take away evil and to make us happy children of God?

THE EDITOR